JLPT N5 VOCAB

DEDICATION

To Kat Woman (Kataoka-Sensei), Gibson-san and Clayton-san. With thanks for those fantastic Tuesday nights in Oita City. Let the love and enthusiasm we shared for JLPT preparation be felt by all who use this text.

JLPT N5 VOCAB

JLPT N5 VOCAB

Japanese Kanji Practice: 102 Kanji (JLPT N5)
Full practice workbook for 102 JLPT N5 Kanji
Available from bookstores and Amazon
ISBN: 978-1-913720-01-8

- Kanji-per-page practice focus
- Japanese and Chinese readings
- 400+ compound Kanji words (jukujo)
- Kanji ordered by common use
- Progressive development of compound Kanji
- Practice tests and consolidation exercises

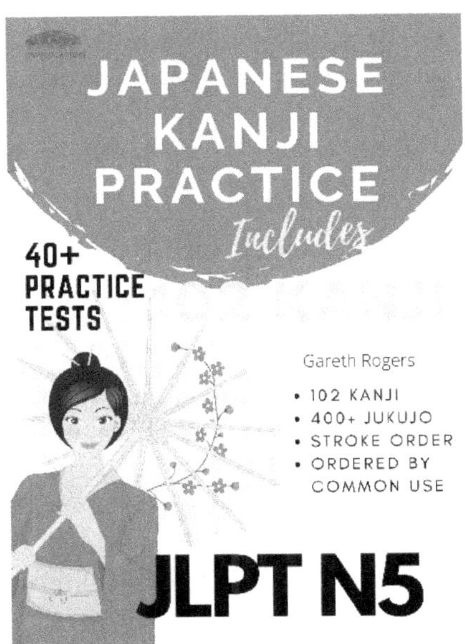

JLPT N5 VOCAB

Cambridge Learning House trades on behalf of
Cambridge Press Ltd
71-75 Shelton Street,
Covent Garden,
London,
England, WC2H 9JQ

Email: enquiries@cambridgepress.co.uk
Website: www.cambridgepress.co.uk

ISBN: 978-1-913720-00-1

The kanji and vocabulary included are the expected requirements of the JLPT N5. Neither the author nor publisher can guarantee that all vocabulary included in this text will appear in the JLPT assessment. Neither can the author or publisher assure that additional vocabulary and kanji absent from this edition will or will not be featured in JLPT assessment. All vocabulary and kanji included have been selected following analysis of typical patterns of vocabulary usage in previous JLPT assessment papers. The content is not endorsed by the JLPT administration.

JLPT N5 VOCAB

How to use this book

Kanji	Furigana	Romaji	English	✓
動物	どうぶつ	doubutsu	animal	
鳥	とり	tori	bird	

Kanji is only written with the vocabulary if it is a Kanji you may be expected to know at this level.

The **Furigana** displays the vocabulary written in Japanese using hiragana or katakana.

The **Romaji** gives the romanised phonetic sound.

English gives the meaning of the vocabulary in English.

The check box at the end can be used to record when you are confident that you have memorised the vocabulary.

Testing yourself with the 89 Practice Quizzes

1. **Learn** – look at the vocabulary list on the left hand page
2. **Cover** – Cover the vocabulary list on the left hand page
3. **Write** – Write out the answers in the practice quiz
4. **Check** – Check how well you did! Try again if you need

JLPT N5 VOCAB

Contents

SECTION 1
N5 VOCABULARY
A- Z of Topics

Animals

Kanji	Furigana	Romaji	English	✓
動物	どうぶつ	doubutsu	animal	
鳥	とり	tori	bird	
猫		neko	cat	
犬		inu	dog	

Practice Quiz 1 - Animals

Kanji	Furigana	Romaji	English	✓
動物			animal	
鳥			bird	
			cat	
			dog	

Body

Kanji	Furigana	Romaji	English	✓
足	あし	ashi	leg, foot	
頭	あたま	atama	head	
顔	かお	kao	face	
体	からだ	karada	body	
口	くち	kuchi	mouth	
声	こえ	koe	voice	
耳	みみ	mimi	ear	
目	め	me	eye	
	おなか	onaka	stomach	
	て	te	hand	
	は	ha	teeth	
	はな	hana	nose	

Practice Quiz 2 - Body

Kanji	Furigana	Romaji	English	✓
足			leg, foot	
頭			head	
顔			face	
体			body	
口			mouth	
声			voice	
耳			ear	
目			eye	
			stomach	
			hand	
			teeth	
			nose	

Cleaning

Kanji	Furigana	Romaji	English	✓
石鹸	せっけん	sekken	soap	
	あびる	abiru	to take a shower	
	あらう	arau	to wash	
	きれい	kirei	beautiful, clean	
	そうじ	souji	to clean	
	はれる	hareru	to clear up	
	みがく	migaku	to polish, to brush	

JLPT N5 VOCAB

Practice Quiz 3 - Cleaning

Kanji	Furigana	Romaji	English	✓
石鹸			soap	
			to take a shower	
			to wash	
			beautiful, clean	
			to clean	
			to clear up	
			to polish, to brush	

Clothing

Kanji	Furigana	Romaji	English	✓
上着	うわぎ	uwagi	coat, jacket	
	かける	kakeru	to wear	
	かぶる	kaburu	to put on a hat	
	きる	kiru	to wear, put on	
	くつ	kutsu	shoe	
	くつした	kutsushita	socks	
	コート	kooto	coat	
	シャツ	shatsu	shirt	
	スカート	sukaato	skirt	
	ズボン	zubon	trousers	
	スリッパ	surippa	slipper	

Practice Quiz 4 - Clothing

Kanji	Furigana	Romaji	English	✓
上着			coat, jacket	
			to wear	
			to put on a hat	
			to wear, put on	
			shoe	
			socks	
			coat	
			shirt	
			skirt	
			trousers	
			slipper	

Clothing Part 2

Kanji	Furigana	Romaji	English	✓
	セーター	seetaa	sweater	
	せびろ	sebiro	jacket, suit	
	せんたく	sentaku	washing, to wash	
	ぬぐ	nugu	to take off	
	ネクタイ	nekutai	necktie	
	はく	haku	to put on shoes	
	ふく	fuku	clothes	
	ぼうし	boushi	hat	
	ポケット	poketto	pocket	
	ボタン	botan	button	
	ようふく	youfuku	western clothing	

Practice Quiz 5 – Clothing Part 2

Kanji	Furigana	Romaji	English	✓
			sweater	
			jacket, suit	
			washing, to wash	
			to take off	
			necktie	
			to put on shoes	
			clothes	
			hat	
			pocket	
			button	
			western clothing	

Colours

Kanji	Furigana	Romaji	English	✓
青い	あおい	aoi	blue	
赤い	あかい	akai	red	
	いろ	iro	colour	
	くろい	kuroi	black	
	しろい	shiroi	white	
	ちゃいろ	chairo	brown	
	きいろい	kiiroi	yellow	
	みどり	midori	green	

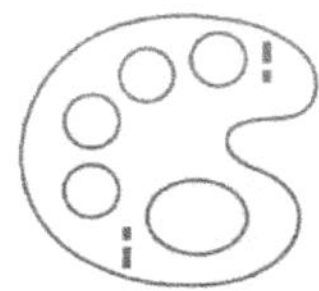

Practice Quiz 6 - Colours

Kanji	Furigana	Romaji	English	✓
青い			blue	
赤い			red	
			colour	
			black	
			white	
			brown	
			yellow	
			green	

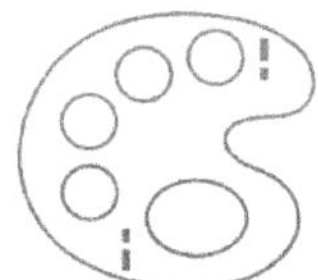

 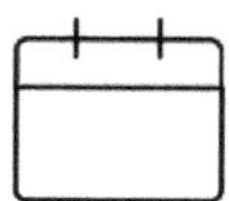

JLPT N5 VOCAB

Days of the Week

Kanji	Furigana	Romaji	English	✓
月曜日	げつようび	getsuyoubi	Monday	
火曜日	かようび	kayoubi	Tuesday	
水曜日	すいようび	suiyoubi	Wednesday	
木曜日	もくようび	mokuyoubi	Thursday	
金曜日	きんようび	kinyoubi	Friday	
土曜日	どようび	doyoubi	Saturday	
日曜日	にちようび	nichiyoubi	Sunday	

Additional:

Furigana	Romaji	English	✓
いちにち	ichinichi	one day	
きょう	kyou	today	
まいにち	mainichi	every day	

JLPT N5 VOCAB

Practice Quiz 7 – Days of the Week

Kanji	Furigana	Romaji	English	✓
月曜日			Monday	
火曜日			Tuesday	
水曜日			Wednesday	
木曜日			Thursday	
金曜日			Friday	
土曜日			Saturday	
日曜日			Sunday	

Additional:

Furigana	Romaji	English	✓
		one day	
		today	
		every day	

Directions

Kanji	Furigana	Romaji	English	✓
	まっすぐに	massugu ni	straight ahead	
	きた	kita	north	
	にし	nishi	west	
左	ひだり	hidari	left	
右	みぎ	migi	right	
	みなみ	minami	south	
東	ひがし	higashi	east	

Practice Quiz 8 - Directions

Kanji	Furigana	Romaji	English	✓
			straight ahead	
			north	
			west	
左			left	
右			right	
			south	
東			east	

JLPT N5 VOCAB

Drinks

Kanji	Furigana	Romaji	English	✓
お茶	おちゃ	ocha	tea	
牛乳	ぎゅうにゅう	gyuunyuu	milk	
飲物	のみもの	nomimono	drinks	
	おさけ	osake	alcohol, sake	
	きっさてん	kissaten	coffee shop	
	のむ	nomu	to drink	
	おみず	omizu	water	

Practice Quiz 9 - Drinks

Kanji	Furigana	Romaji	English	✓
お茶			tea	
牛乳			milk	
飲物			drinks	
			alcohol, sake	
			coffee shop	
			to drink	
			water	

Every Day

Kanji	Furigana	Romaji	English	✓
朝	あさ	asa	morning	
今朝	けさ	kesa	this morning	
	ごご	gogo	afternoon	
午前	ごぜん	gozen	morning, a.m.	
昼	ひる	hiru	noon	
	こんばん	konban	this evening	
	ばん	ban	Evening	
	まいあさ	maiasa	every morning	
	まいばん	maiban	every evening	

Practice Quiz 10 – Every Day

Kanji	Furigana	Romaji	English	✓
朝			morning	
今朝			this morning	
			afternoon	
午前			morning, a.m.	
昼			noon	
			this evening	
			Evening	
			every morning	
			every evening	

JLPT N5 VOCAB

Family

Kanji	Furigana	Romaji	English	✓
	あに	ani	older brother	
	あね	ane	older sister	
	いもうと	imouto	someone's younger sister	
	おとうと	otouto	someone's younger brother	
	かぞく	kazoku	family	
	かない	kanai	my wife	
	きょうだい	kyoudai	siblings	
	けっこん	kekkon	marriage	
	ごしゅじん	goshujin	someone else's husband	
父	ちち	chichi	my father	
	ともだち	tomodachi	friend	

JLPT N5 VOCAB

Practice Quiz 11 - Family

Kanji	Furigana	Romaji	English	✓
			older brother	
			older sister	
			someone's younger sister	
			someone's younger brother	
			family	
			my wife	
			siblings	
			marriage	
			someone else's husband	
父			my father	
			friend	

Family Part 2

Kanji	Furigana	Romaji	English	✓
母	はは	haha	my mother	
	おかあさん	okaasan	my own mother	
	おくさん	okusan	someone's wife	
	おじさん	ojisan	uncle	
	おじいさん	ojiisan	grand father	
	おとうさん	otousan	father	
	おにいさん	oniisan	someone's elder brother	
	おねえさん	oneesan	someone's elder sister	
	おばさん	obasan	aunt	
	おばあさん	obaasan	grandmother	
	りょうしん	ryoushin	parents	

Practice Quiz 12 - Family

Kanji	Furigana	Romaji	English	✓
母			my mother	
			my own mother	
			someone's wife	
			uncle	
			grand father	
			father	
			someone's elder brother	
			someone's elder sister	
			aunt	
			grandmother	
			parents	

Feelings

Kanji	Furigana	Romaji	English	✓
	いい / よい	ii, yoi	good	
	かぜ	kaze	a cold	
	さむい	samui	cold	
	すずしい	suzushii	cool	
	たのしい	tanoshii	pleasant, enjoyable	
	つまらない	tsumaranai	uninteresting	
	びょうき	byouki	ill, sick	

Practice Quiz 13 - Feelings

Kanji	Furigana	Romaji	English	✓
			good	
			a cold	
			cold	
			cool	
			pleasant, enjoyable	
			uninteresting	
			ill, sick	

Feelings Part 2

Kanji	Furigana	Romaji	English	✓
	いや	iya	not likable, unpleasant	
	きらい	kirai	unpleasant, not likable	
	けっこう	kekkou	fine, all right	
	げんき	genki	vigor, health, vitality	
	だいじょうぶ	daijoubu	OK	
	だいすき	daisuki	to be very fond of	
	わるい	warui	bad	
	かわいい	kawaii	cute, pretty	

JLPT N5 VOCAB

Practice Quiz 13 – Feelings Part 2

Kanji	Furigana	Romaji	English	✓
			not likable, unpleasant	
			unpleasant, not likable	
			fine, all right	
			vigor, health, vitality	
			OK	
			to be very fond of	
			bad	
			cute, pretty	

JLPT N5 VOCAB

Food

Kanji	Furigana	Romaji	English	✓
	あまい	amai	sweet	
	あさごはん	asagohan	breakfast	
	おいしい	oishii	tasty, delicious	
	おかし	okashi	confectionary, cake	
	おべんとう	obentou	lunchbox	
	からい	karai	hot, spicy	
	ぎゅうにく	gyuuniku	beef	
	さかな	sakana	fish	
	さとう	satou	sugar	
	たべもの	tabemono	food	

Practice Quiz - 14 - Food

Kanji	Furigana	Romaji	English	✓
			sweet	
			breakfast	
			tasty, delicious	
			confectionary, cake	
			lunchbox	
			hot, spicy	
			beef	
			fish	
			sugar	
			food	

JLPT N5 VOCAB

Food Part 2

Kanji	Furigana	Romaji	English	✓
	ちゃわん	chawan	rice bowl	
	とりにく	toriniku	chicken meat	
	おにく	oniku	meat	
	まずい	mazui	bad tasting	
	やさい	yasai	vegetable	
	くだもの	kudamono	fruit	
	ごはん	gohan	Rice or meal	
	しお	shio	salt	
	しょうゆ	shouyu	soy sauce	
	スプーン	supuun	spoon	
食べる	たべる	taberu	to eat	

Practice Quiz 15 - Food Part 2

Kanji	Furigana	Romaji	English	✓
			rice bowl	
			chicken meat	
			meat	
			bad tasting	
			vegetable	
			fruit	
			Rice or meal	
			salt	
			soy sauce	
			spoon	
食べる			to eat	

Food Part 3

Kanji	Furigana	Romaji	English	✓
	たまご	tamago	egg	
	はし	hashi	chopsticks	
	バター	bataa	butter	
	パン	pan	bread	
	ばんごはん	bangohan	dinner	
	ひるごはん	hirugohan	lunch	
	フォーク	fooku	fork	
	ぶたにく	butaniku	pork	
	りょうり	ryouri	cooking	
	レストラン	resutoran	restaurant	

Practice Quiz 16 - Food Part 3

Kanji	Furigana	Romaji	English	✓
			egg	
			chopsticks	
			butter	
			bread	
			dinner	
			lunch	
			fork	
			pork	
			cooking	
			restaurant	

JLPT N5 VOCAB

Frequency

Kanji	Furigana	Romaji	English	✓
	よく	yoku	often	
	～ずつ	~zutsu	each	
	ぜんぶ	zenbu	all	
	たくさん	takusan	many, much	
	～ど	~do	~times	
	とても	totemo	very much	
	また	mata	also, again	
	もっと	motto	more	
	いつも	itsumo	always	
	ときどき	tokidoki	sometimes	

JLPT N5 VOCAB

Practice Quiz 17 - Frequency

Kanji	Furigana	Romaji	English	✓
			often	
			each	
			all	
			many, much	
			~times	
			very much	
			also, again	
			more	
			always	
			sometimes	

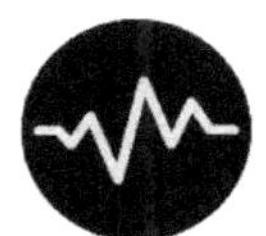

JLPT N5 VOCAB

Home

Kanji	Furigana	Romaji	English	✓
家	いえ	ie	house, home	
	え	e	picture	
	おてあらい	otearai	toilet, lavatory	
	げんかん	genkan	entrance house	
	しゃしん	shashin	photo	
	だいどころ	daidokoro	kitchen	
電気	でんき	denki	electricity	
	はいざら	haizara	ashtray	
	へや	heya	room	
	もん	mon	gate	

Practice Quiz 18 -Home

Kanji	Furigana	Romaji	English	✓
家			house, home	
			picture	
			toilet, lavatory	
			entrance house	
			photo	
			kitchen	
電気			electricity	
			ashtray	
			room	
			gate	

JLPT N5 VOCAB

Home Part 2

Kanji	Furigana	Romaji	English	✓
	アパート	apaato	apartment	
	いす	isu	chair	
	うち	uchi	home	
	かいだん	kaidan	stairs	
	かえる	kaeru	to return home	
	かぎ	kagi	key	
	かびん	kabin	vase	
	テーブル	teeburu	table	
	つくえ	tsukue	desk	
	テレビ	terebi	TV	

JLPT N5 VOCAB

Practice Quiz 19 -Home Part 2

Kanji	Furigana	Romaji	English	✓
			apartment	
			chair	
			home	
			stairs	
			to return home	
			key	
			vase	
			table	
			desk	
			TV	

Home Part 3

Kanji	Furigana	Romaji	English	✓
	と	to	door	
	ドア	doa	door	
	トイレ	toire	toilet, lavatory	
	にわ	niwa	garden	
	おふろ	ofuro	bath	
	ベッド	beddo	bed	
	ほんだな	hondana	bookshelf	
	まど	mado	window	
	レコード	rekoodo	record	

JLPT N5 VOCAB

Practice Quiz 20 -Home Part 3

Kanji	Furigana	Romaji	English	✓
			door	
			door	
			toilet, lavatory	
			garden	
			bath	
			bed	
			bookshelf	
			window	
			record	

Infrastructure

Kanji	Furigana	Romaji	English	✓
	たてもの	tatemono	building	
	はし	hashi	bridge	
	みち	michi	road	
	エレベータ	erebeeta	elevator	
	こうばん	kouban	police box	

Practice Quiz 21 - Infrastructure

Kanji	Furigana	Romaji	English	✓
			building	
			bridge	
			road	
			elevator	
			police box	

Kitchen

Kanji	Furigana	Romaji	English	✓
食堂	しょくどう	shokudou	canteen	
	おさら	osara	plate	
	コップ	koppu	cup, glass	
	ストーブ	sutoobu	stove, heater	
	ナイフ	naifu	knife	
	マッチ	machi	matches	
	れいぞうこ	reizouko	refrigerator	

Practice Quiz 22 - Kitchen

Kanji	Furigana	Romaji	English	✓
食堂			canteen	
			plate	
			cup, glass	
			stove, heater	
			knife	
			matches	
			refrigerator	

Language Terms

Kanji	Furigana	Romaji	English	✓
	えいご	eigo	English language	
	かんじ	kanji	Kanji character	
	ことば	kotoba	phrase, language	
	じしょ	jisho	dictionary	
	しつもん	shitsumon	question	
	じびき	jibiki	dictionary	
手紙	てがみ	tegami	letter	
何	なに	nani	what?	
名前	なまえ	namae	name	
	もんだい	mondai	problem, question	

Practice Quiz 23 -Language Terms

Kanji	Furigana	Romaji	English	✓
			English language	
			Kanji character	
			phrase, language	
			dictionary	
			question	
			dictionary	
手紙			letter	
何			what?	
名前			name	
			problem, question	

Language Terms Part 2

Kanji	Furigana	Romaji	English	✓
	ああ	ah	Ah!	
	あの	ano	well, then	
	あまり	amari	not so	
	ある	aru	to be, to exist	
	いいえ	iie	no	
	いろいろ	iroiro	various	
	ええ	ee	Yes, I see	
	お	o	honorific prefix	
	おなじ	onaji	same	
	かたかな	katakana	Katakana	
	ください	kudasai	give me...	

JLPT N5 VOCAB

Practice Quiz 24 - Language Terms Part 2

Kanji	Furigana	Romaji	English	✓
			Ah!	
			well, then	
			not so	
			to be, to exist	
			no	
			various	
			Yes, I see	
			honorific prefix	
			same	
			Katakana	
			give me...	

JLPT N5 VOCAB

Language Terms Part 3

Kanji	Furigana	Romaji	English	✓
	～ご	~go	~ language	
	しかし	shikashi	however, but	
	じゃ	ja	well, then	
	そう	sou	so	
	そうして	soushite	and then	
	それでは	soredewa	then, well	
	では	dewa	then, well	
	でも	demo	but	
	どう	dou	how?	
	どうして	doushite	why?	

Practice Quiz 25 - Language Terms Part 3

Kanji	Furigana	Romaji	English	✓
			~ language	
			however, but	
			well, then	
			so	
			and then	
			then, well	
			then, well	
			but	
			how?	
			why?	

 # JLPT N5 VOCAB

Language Terms Part 4

Kanji	Furigana	Romaji	English	✓
	どちら	dochira	which, where	
	どの	dono	which?	
	どれ	dore	which?	
	どんな	donna	what kind of?	
	はなし	hanashi	story	
	はなす	hanasu	to talk, to speak	
	ひらがな	hiragana	hiragana	
	ほんとうに	hontou ni	really	
	もしもし	moshimoshi	hello on the phone	
	もちろん	mochiron	of course	

Practice Quiz 26 - -Language Terms Part 4

Kanji	Furigana	Romaji	English	✓
			which, where	
			which?	
			which?	
			what kind of?	
			story	
			to talk, to speak	
			hiragana	
			really	
			hello on the phone	
			of course	

JLPT N5 VOCAB

Measures

Kanji	Furigana	Romaji	English	✓
	キロ	kiro	kg	
	キロ	kiro	km	
	グラム	guramu	gram	
	せい	sei	height	
	メートル	meetoru	meter	
	あつい	atsui	thick	
大きい	おおきい	ookii	big	
小さい	ちいさい	chiisai	small	
	みじかい	mijikai	short	
	すこし	sukoshi	a little	
	ちょっと	chotto	a little	

Practice Quiz 27 - -Measures

Kanji	Furigana	Romaji	English	✓
			kg	
			km	
			gram	
			height	
			meter	
			thick	
大きい			big	
小さい			small	
			short	
			a little	
			a little	

 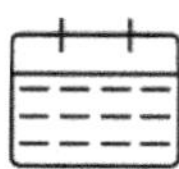

JLPT N5 VOCAB

Months of the Year

Kan	Furigana	Romaji	English	✓
	いちがつ	ichigatsu	January	
	にがつ	nigatsu	February	
	さんがつ	sangatsu	March	
	しがつ	shigatsu	April	
	ごがつ	gogatsu	May	
	ろくがつ	rokugatsu	June	
	しちがつ	shichigatsu	July	
	はちがつ	hachigatsu	August	
	くがつ	kugatsu	September	
	じゅう がつ	juugatsu	October	
	じゅういちがつ	juuichigatsu	November	
	じゅうにがつ	juunigatsu	December	

 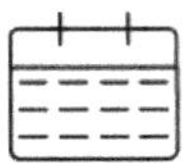

JLPT N5 VOCAB

Practice Quiz 28 - Months of the Year

Kan	Furigana	Romaji	English	✓
			January	
			February	
			March	
			April	
			May	
			June	
			July	
			August	
			September	
			October	
			November	
			December	

JLPT N5 VOCAB

Month (by days)

Kanji	Furigana	Romaji	English	✓
	ついたち	tsuitachi	the 1st day of a month	
	ふつか	futsuka	2nd day of the month, 2 days	
	みっか	mikka	3rd day of a month, 3 days	
	よっか	yokka	4th day of the month, 4 days	
	いつか	itsuka	the 5th day of the month, 5 days	
	むいか	muika	the 6th day of a month, 6 days	
	なのか	nanoka	the 7th of a month,	
	ようか	youka	8th day of the month, 8 days	
	ここのか	kokonoka	9th day of a month, 9 days	
	とおか	tooka	the 10th day of a month, 10 days	

Practice Quiz 29 - Month (by days)

Kanji	Furigana	Romaji	English	✓
			the 1st day of a month	
			2nd day of the month, 2 days	
			3rd day of a month, 3 days	
			4th day of the month, 4 days	
			the 5th day of the month, 5 days	
			the 6th day of a month, 6 days	
			the 7th of a month,	
			8th day of the month, 8 days	
			9th day of a month, 9 days	
			the 10th day of a month, 10 days	

JLPT N5 VOCAB

Month (other times)

Kanji	Furigana	Romaji	English	✓
	ひとつき	hitotsuki	one month	
	まいつき/ まいげつ	maitsuki/ maigetsu	every month	
	らいげつ	raigetsu	next month	
	〜かげつ	~kagetsu	~ number months	
	カレンダー	karendaa	calendar	
	こんげつ	kongetsu	this month	
	せんげつ	sengetsu	last month	

Prxtice Quiz 30 - Month (other times)

Kanji	Furigana	Romaji	English	✓
			one month	
			every month	
			next month	
			~ number months	
			calendar	
			this month	
			last month	

Nature

Kanji	Furigana	Romaji	English	✓
	いけ	ike	pond	
	うみ	umi	sea	
川	かわ	kawa	river	
空	そら	sora	sky	
木	き	ki	tree	
花	はな	hana	flower	
	やま	yama	mountain	
	さく	saku	to blossom	

Practice Quiz 31 – Nature

Kanji	Furigana	Romaji	English	✓
			pond	
			sea	
川			river	
空			sky	
木			tree	
花			flower	
			mountain	
			to blossom	

JLPT N5 VOCAB

Numbers

Kanji	Furigana	Romaji	English	✓
	ゼロ	zero	zero	
一	いち	ichi	one	
二	に	ni	two	
三	さん	san	three	
四	し	shi	four	
五	ご	go	five	
六	ろく	roku	six	
七	ななつ	nanatsu	seven	
八	はち	hachi	eight	
九	きゅう	kyuu	nine	
九	く	ku	nine	
十	じゅう	juu	ten	

JLPT N5 VOCAB

Practice Quiz 32 - Numbers

Kanji	Furigana	Romaji	English	✓
			zero	
一			one	
二			two	
三			three	
四			four	
五			five	
六			six	
七			seven	
八			eight	
九			nine	
九			nine	
十			ten	

JLPT N5 VOCAB

Number Part 2

Kanji	Furigana	Romaji	English	✓
	せん	sen	1,000, thousand	
	ばんごう	bangou	number	
百	ひゃく	hyaku	hundred	
万	まん	man	ten thousand	
	いくつ	ikutsu	how many, how old	
	いくら	ikura	how much	
	いちばん	ichiban	the best, the first	

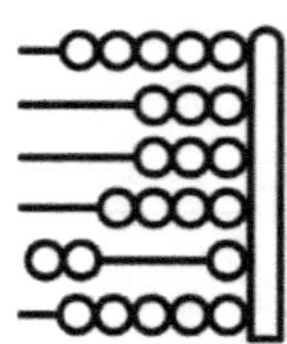

Practie Quiz 33 - Number Part 2

Kanji	Furigana	Romaji	English	✓
			1,000, thousand	
			number	
百			hundred	
万			ten thousand	
			how many, how old	
			how much	
			the best, the first	

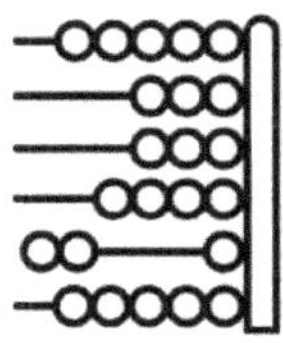

Number Part 3 (Counting)

Kanji	Furigana	Romaji	English	✓
	れい	rei	zero	
	ひとつ	hitotsu	one	
	ふたつ	futatsu	two	
	みっつ	mittsu	three	
	よっつ	yottsu	four	
	いつつ	itsutsu	five	
	むっつ	muttsu	six	
	やっつ	yattsu	eight	
	ここのつ	kokonotsu	nine	
	とう	tou	ten	

Practice Quiz 34 - Number Part 3 (Counting)

Kanji	Furigana	Romaji	English	✓
			zero	
			one	
			two	
			three	
			four	
			five	
			six	
			eight	
			nine	
			ten	

Number (Counters)

Kanji	Furigana	Romaji	English	✓
	〜ひき	~hiki	counter for animals	
	〜だい	~dai	counter for machines	
	〜はい	~hai	cups of ~	
	~ほん	~hon	counter for long objects	

Practice Quiz 35 - Number (Counters)

Kanji	Furigana	Romaji	English	✓
			counter for animals	
			counter for machines	
			cups of ~	
			counter for long objects	

JLPT N5 VOCAB

Office

Kanji	Furigana	Romaji	English	✓
紙	かみ	kami	paper	
	きって	kitte	stamp	
	しごと	shigoto	work	
電話	でんわ	denwa	phone	
葉書	はがき	hagaki	postcard	
	かける	kakeru	to make a phone call	
	はたらく	hataraku	to work	
	ふうとう	fuutou	envelope	
	いそがしい	isogashii	to be busy	
	つとめる	tsutomeru	to work for someone	

JLPT N5 VOCAB

Practice Quiz 36 - Office

Kanji	Furigana	Romaji	English	✓
紙			paper	
			stamp	
			work	
電話			phone	
葉書			postcard	
			to make a phone call	
			to work	
			envelope	
			to be busy	
			to work for someone	

JLPT N5 VOCAB

People

Kanji	Furigana	Romaji	English	✓
女	おんな	onna	woman	
	~にん	~nin	... people	
	ひとり	hitori	one person	
	ふたり	futari	two people	
	みなさん	minsan	everyone	
	みんな	minna	all, everyone	
外国人	がいこくじん	gaikokujin	foreigner	

Practice Quiz 37 - People

Kanji	Furigana	Romaji	English	✓
女			woman	
			... people	
			one person	
			two people	
			everyone	
			all, everyone	
外国人			foreigner	

JLPT N5 VOCAB

People 2

Kanji	Furigana	Romaji	English	✓
	うまれる	umareru	to be born	
	あなた	anata	you	
男	おとこ	otoko	man	
男の子	おとこのこ	otokonoko	boy	
大人	おとな	otona	adult	
女の子	おんなのこ	onnanoko	girl	
学生	がくせい	gakusei	student	
	こども	kodomo	child	

Practice Quiz 38 - People 2

Kanji	Furigana	Romaji	English	✓
			to be born	
			you	
男			man	
男の子			boy	
大人			adult	
女の子			girl	
学生			student	
			child	

People 3

Kanji	Furigana	Romaji	English	✓
人	ひと	hito	person	
	わたし	watashi	me, I	
	おおぜい	oozei	many people	
	かた	kata	person (polite)	
	～さん	~san	Mr., Mrs.	
	じぶん	jibun	oneself	
	だれ	dare	who?	
	なる	naru	to become	

Practice Quiz 39 - People 3

Kanji	Furigana	Romaji	English	✓
人			person	
			me, I	
			many people	
			person (polite)	
			Mr., Mrs.	
			oneself	
			who?	
			to become	

Places

Kanji	Furigana	Romaji	English	✓
銀行	ぎんこう	ginkou	bank	
	こうえん	kouen	park, large garden	
	あそこ	asoko	over there	
駅	えき	eki	station	
	かど	kado	corner	
外	そと	soto	outside	
	ところ	tokoro	place	
	としょかん	toshokan	library	

JLPT N5 VOCAB

Practice Quiz 40 - Places

Kanji	Furigana	Romaji	English	✓
銀行			bank	
			park, large garden	
			over there	
駅			station	
			corner	
外			outside	
			place	
			library	

Places 2

Kanji	Furigana	Romaji	English	✓
	まち	machi	city, town	
	みせ	mise	shop	
	ここ	koko	here	
	どこ	doko	where?	
	びょういん	byouin	hospital	
	ホテル	hoteru	hotel	
	～や	~ya	shop. store	
	やおや	yaoya	vegetable shop	

JLPT N5 VOCAB

Practice Quiz 41 - Places 2

Kanji	Furigana	Romaji	English	✓
			city, town	
			shop	
			here	
			where?	
			hospital	
			hotel	
			shop. store	
			vegetable shop	

Positions

Kanji	Furigana	Romaji	English	✓
	うえ	ue	top, on, above	
	した	shita	under, below	
近い	ちかい	chikai	near, close	
	とおい	tooi	far	
中	なか	naka	inside	
前	まえ	mae	front	
	よる	yoru	night	
	あちら	achira	over there (polite)	

Practice Quiz 42 - Positions

Kanji	Furigana	Romaji	English	✓
			top, on, above	
			under, below	
近い			near, close	
			far	
中			inside	
前			front	
			night	
			over there (polite)	

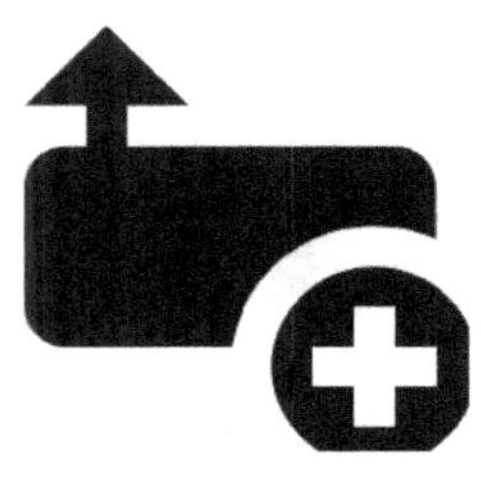

Positions 2

Kanji	Furigana	Romaji	English	✓
	あの	ano	that (over there)	
	あれ	are	that one	
	うしろ	ushiro	rear, behind	
	こちら	kochira	this side, this place	
	この	kono	this...	
	そこ	soko	there	
	そちら	sochira	there (polite)	
	その	sono	that...	

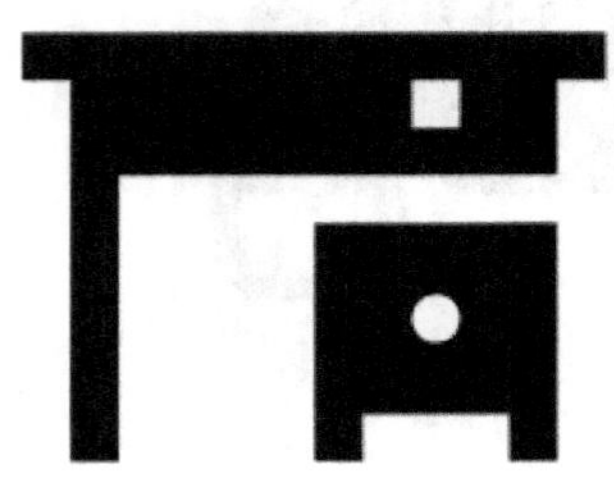

Practice Quiz 43 - Positions 2

Kanji	Furigana	Romaji	English	✓
			that (over there)	
			that one	
			rear, behind	
			this side, this place	
			this...	
			there	
			there (polite)	
			that...	

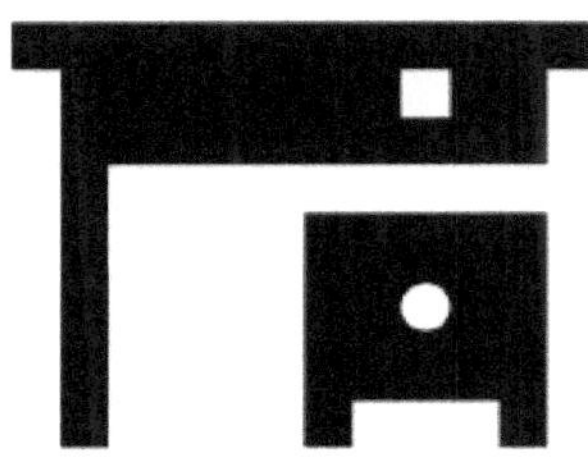

JLPT N5 VOCAB

Positions 3

Kanji	Furigana	Romaji	English	✓
	そば	soba	next to	
	それ	sore	that	
	となり	tonari	next to	
	ひがし	higashi	east	
	～まえ	~mae	before, in front of	
	むこう	mukou	over there	
入口	いりぐち	iriguchi	entrance	

JLPT N5 VOCAB

Practice Quiz 44 - Positions 3

Kanji	Furigana	Romaji	English	✓
			next to	
			that	
			next to	
			east	
			before, in front of	
			over there	
入口			entrance	

JLPT N5 VOCAB

School

Kanji	Furigana	Romaji	English	✓
	きょうしつ	kyoushitsu	class room	
	じゅぎょう	jugyou	lesson, class	
	しゅくだい	shukudai	homework	
	せいと	seito	student	
先生	せんせい	sensei	teacher	
大学	だいがく	daigaku	university	
	べんきょう	benkyou	to study	
本	ほん	hon	book	
	れんしゅう	renshuu	practice	

Practice Quiz 45 - School

Kanji	Furigana	Romaji	English	✓
			class room	
			lesson, class	
			homework	
			student	
先生			teacher	
大学			university	
			to study	
本			book	
			practice	

School Part 2

Kanji	Furigana	Romaji	English	✓
	えんぴつ	enpitsu	pencil	
	おぼえる	oboeru	to memorize	
	かく	kaku	to write	
	がっこう	gakkou	school	
	かばん	kaban	bag	
	クラス	kurasu	class	
	こたえる	kotaeru	to answer	
	さくぶん	sakubun	composition	

Practice Quiz 46 - School Part 2

Kanji	Furigana	Romaji	English	✓
			pencil	
			to memorize	
			to write	
			school	
			bag	
			class	
			to answer	
			composition	

School Part 3

Kanji	Furigana	Romaji	English	✓
	テープ	teepu	tape	
	テープレコーダー	teepu rekoodaa	tape recorder	
	しる	shiru	to know	
	すわる	suwaru	to sit	
	テスト	tesuto	test	
	ならう	narau	to learn	
	ならぶ	narabu	to form a line	

 **JLPT N5 VOCAB**

Practice quiz 47 - School Part 3

Kanji	Furigana	Romaji	English	✓
			tape	
			tape recorder	
			to know	
			to sit	
			test	
			to learn	
			to form a line	

JLPT N5 VOCAB

School Part 4

Kanji	Furigana	Romaji	English	✓
	ならべる	naraberu	to line up	
	ノート	nooto	notebook	
	ページ	peeji	page	
	ぺん	pen	pen	
	ボールペン	boorupen	ballpen	
	まんねんひつ	mannenhitsu	fountain pen	
	よむ	yomu	to read	
	りゅうがくせい	ryuugakusei	foreign student	

Practice Quiz 48 - School Part 4

Kanji	Furigana	Romaji	English	✓
			to line up	
			notebook	
			page	
			pen	
			ballpen	
			fountain pen	
			to read	
			foreign student	

JLPT N5 VOCAB

Seasons

Kanji	Furigana	Romaji	English	✓
	あき	aki	autumn, fall	
夏	なつ	natsu	summer	
	なつやすみ	natsuyasumi	summer vacation	
	はる	haru	spring	

Practice Quiz 49 - Seasons

Kanji	Furigana	Romaji	English	✓
			autumn, fall	
夏			summer	
			summer vacation	
			spring	

JLPT N5 VOCAB

Shopping

Kanji	Furigana	Romaji	English	✓
	かいもの	kaimono	shopping	
	うる	uru	to sell	
	かう	kau	to buy	
	かえす	kaesu	to return an object	
	デパート	depaato	department store	

Practice Quiz 50 - Shopping

Kanji	Furigana	Romaji	English	✓
			shopping	
			to sell	
			to buy	
			to return an object	
			department store	

Temperature

Kanji	Furigana	Romaji	English	✓
温かい	あたたかい	atatakai	warm	
暑い	あつい	atsui	hot (air)	
冷たい	つめたい	tsumetai	cold	

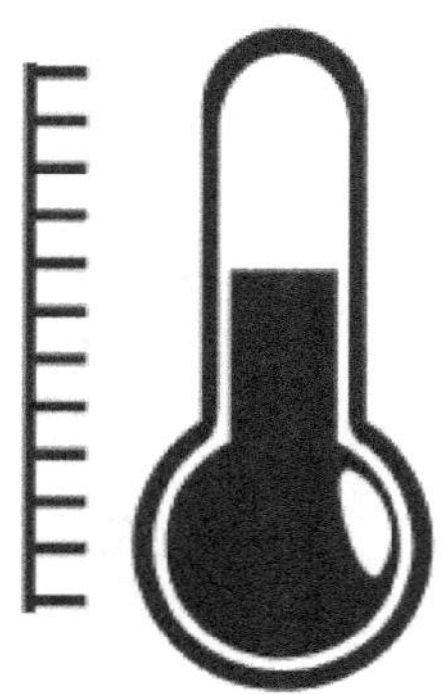

Practice Quiz 51 - Temperature

Kanji	Furigana	Romaji	English	✓
温かい			warm	
暑い			hot (air)	
冷たい			cold	

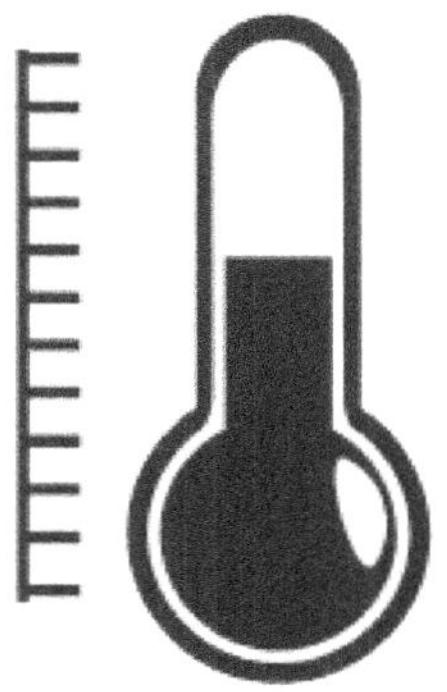

JLPT N5 VOCAB

Time

Kanji	Furigana	Romaji	English	✓
古い	ふるい	furui	old	
	いつ	itsu	when	
	おわる	owaru	to end	
	かかる	kakaru	to take time	
	ぐらい	gurai	about	
	～じ	~ji	o'clock	
	～すぎ	~sugi	past, over	
	すぐに	sugu ni	at once	
	ねる	neru	to go to bed	

JLPT N5 VOCAB

Practice Quiz 52 - Time

Kanji	Furigana	Romaji	English	✓
古い			old	
			when	
			to end	
			to take time	
			about	
			o'clock	
			past, over	
			at once	
	ねる	neru	to go to bed	

Time Part 2

Kanji	Furigana	Romaji	English	✓
後	あと	ato	later, after	
今	いま	ima	now	
	おそい	osoi	late, slow	
	きょねん	kyonen	last year	
	さき	saki	earlier, former	
	じかん	jikan	time	
	～じかん	~jikan	~hours (classificator)	
時計	とけい	tokei	watch, clock	
	はやい	hayai	early	
	それから	sorekara	after that	
	もう	mou	already, yet	

Practice Quiz 53 - Time Part

Kanji	Furigana	Romaji	English	✓
後			later, after	
今			now	
			late, slow	
			last year	
			earlier, former	
			time	
			~hours (classificator)	
時計			watch, clock	
			early	
			after that	
			already, yet	

JLPT N5 VOCAB

Travel

Kanji	Furigana	Romaji	English	✓
外国	がいこく	gaikoku	foreign country	
	きっぷ	kippu	ticket	
国	くに	kuni	country	
車	くるま	kuruma	car	
	じてんしゃ	jitensha	bicycle	
	じどうしゃ	jidousha	car, vehicle	
	たいしかん	taishikan	embassy	
	ちかてつ	chikatetsu	subway	
	ちず	chizu	map	
電車	でんしゃ	densha	train	
	やすみ	yasumi	holiday, vacation	

JLPT N5 VOCAB

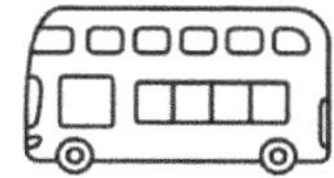

Practice Quiz 54 - Travel

Kanji	Furigana	Romaji	English	✓
外国			foreign country	
			ticket	
国			country	
車			car	
			bicycle	
			car, vehicle	
			embassy	
			subway	
			map	
電車			train	
			holiday, vacation	

Travel Part 2

Kanji	Furigana	Romaji	English	✓
	りょこう	ryokou	travel	
	いく	iku	to go	
	おりる	oriru	to get off	
	しめる	shimeru	to fasten a seatbelt	
	～じん	~jin	~an, ~ese (nationality)	
	タクシー	takushii	taxi	
	にもつ	nimotsu	luggage	
	のぼる	noboru	to climb up	
	のる	noru	to take, to ride	
	バス	basu	bus	
	ひこうき	hikouki	plane	

Practice Quiz 55 - Travel Part 2

Kanji	Furigana	Romaji	English	✓
			travel	
			to go	
			to get off	
			to fasten a seatbelt	
			~an, ~ese (nationality)	
			taxi	
			luggage	
			to climb up	
			to take, to ride	
			bus	
			plane	

Weather

Kanji	Furigana	Romaji	English	✓
雨	あめ	ame	rain	
	かぜ	kaze	wind	
天気	てんき	tenki	weather	
	かさ	kasa	umbrella	
	くもり	kumori	cloudy weather	
	さす	sasu	to open an umbrella	
	ふく	fuku	to blow (wind)	
	ふる	furu	to fall (rain, snow)	

Practice Quiz 56 - Weather

Kanji	Furigana	Romaji	English	✓
雨			rain	
			wind	
天気			weather	
			umbrella	
			cloudy weather	
			to open an umbrella	
			to blow (wind)	
			to fall (rain, snow)	

Week

Kanji	Furigana	Romaji	English	✓
	こんしゅう	konshuu	this week	
	〜しゅうかん	~shuukan	... weeks	
	せんしゅう	senshuu	last week	
	まいしゅう	maishuu	every week	
	らいしゅう	raishuu	next week	

Practice Quiz 57 - Week

Kanji	Furigana	Romaji	English	✓
			this week	
			... weeks	
			last week	
			every week	
			next week	

Year

Kanji	Furigana	Romaji	English	✓
今年	ことし	kotoshi	this year	
	おととし	ototoshi	the year before last	
	さらいねん	sarainen	the year after next year	
	～ねん	~nen	~years	
	まいとし/ まいねん	maitoshi/ mainen	every year	
	らいねん	rainen	next year	

Practice Quiz 58 - Year

Kanji	Furigana	Romaji	English	✓
今年			this year	
			the year before last	
			the year after next year	
			~years	
			every year	
			next year	

SECTION 2
N5 VOCABULARY

い Adjectives

Adjectives (1-10)

Furigana	Romaji	English	✓
あおい	aoi	blue	
あかい	akai	red	
あかるい	akarui	light, bright	
あたたかい	atatakai	warm	
あたらしい	atarashii	new	
あつい	atsui	thick	
あつい	atsui	hot (air)	
あぶない	abunai	dangerous	
あまい	amai	sweet	
いい / よい	ii, yoi	good	

Practice Quiz 59 - Adjectives (1-10)

Furigana	Romaji	English	✓
		blue	
		red	
		light, bright	
		warm	
		new	
		thick	
		hot (air)	
		dangerous	
		sweet	
		good	

JLPT N5 VOCAB

Adjectives (11-20)

Hurigana	Romaji	English	✓
いそがしい	isogashii	to be busy	
いたい	itai	to be painful	
うすい	Usui	thin	
おいしい	oishii	tasty, delicious	
おおきい	ookii	big	
おそい	osoi	late, slow	
おもい	omoi	heavy	
おもしろい	omoshiroi	interesting, funny	
からい	karai	hot, spicy	
かるい	karui	light (not heavy)	

Practice Quiz 60 - Adjectives (11-20)

Hurigana	Romaji	English	✓
		to be busy	
		to be painful	
		thin	
		tasty, delicious	
		big	
		late, slow	
		heavy	
		interesting, funny	
		hot, spicy	
		light (not heavy)	

Adjectives (21-30)

Furigana	Romaji	English	✓
きいろい	kiiroi	yellow	
きたない	kitanai	dirty	
きらい	kirai	unpleasant, not likable	
きれい	kirei	beautiful, clean	
くもり	kumori	cloudy weather	
くらい	Kurai	dark	
けっこう	kekkou	fine, all right	
さむい	samui	cold	
せまい	semai	narrow	
せまい	semai	narrow	

JLPT N5 VOCAB

Practice Quiz 61 - Adjectives (21-30)

Furigana	Romaji	English	✓
		yellow	
		dirty	
		unpleasant, not likable	
		beautiful, clean	
		cloudy weather	
		dark	
		fine, all right	
		cold	
		narrow	
		narrow	

JLPT N5 VOCAB

Adjectives (31-40)

Furigana	Romaji	English	✓
せまい	semai	narrow	
たかい	takai	high, expensive	
たのしい	tanoshii	pleasant, enjoyable	
ちいさい	chiisai	small	
ちかい	chikai	near, close	
ちゃいろ	chairo	brown	
つまらない	tsumaranai	uninteresting	
つめたい	tsumetai	cold	
つまらない	tsumaranai	uninteresting	
つめたい	tsumetai	cold	

Practice Quiz 62 - Adjectives (31-40)

Furigana	Romaji	English	✓
		narrow	
		high, expensive	
		pleasant, enjoyable	
		small	
		near, close	
		brown	
		uninteresting	
		cold	
		uninteresting	
		cold	

JLPT N5 VOCAB

Adjectives (41-50)

Furigana	Romaji	English	✓
つよい	tsuyoi	strong	
とおい	tooi	far	
ながい	nagai	long	
はやい	hayai	fast, quick	
はやい	hayai	early	
ひくい	hikui	low	
ひろい	hiroi	wide, spacious	
ふとい	futoi	thick, fat	
ふるい	furui	old	
ほしい	hoshii	to want something	

Practice Quiz 63 - Adjectives (41-50)

Furigana	Romaji	English	✓
		strong	
		far	
		long	
		fast, quick	
		early	
		low	
		wide, spacious	
		thick, fat	
		old	
		to want something	

Adjectives (51 – 59)

Furigana	Romaji	English	✓
ほそい	hosoi	thin, fine	
まずい	mazui	bad tasting	
まるい	marui	round	
みじかい	mijikai	short	
むずかしい	muzukashii	difficult	
やさしい	yasashii	gentle	
やすい	yasui	cheap, inexpensive	
わかい	wakai	young	
わるい	warui	bad	

Practice Quiz 64 - Adjectives (51 – 59)

Furigana	Romaji	English	✓
		thin, fine	
		bad tasting	
		round	
		short	
		difficult	
		gentle	
		cheap, inexpensive	
		young	
		bad	

JLPT N5 VOCAB

SECTION 3
N5 VOCABULARY
な Adjectives

JLPT N5 VOCAB

な adjectives for N5 (1 -10)

Hiragana	Romaji	Meaning	✓
すき	Suki	To like,love	
けっこう	Kekkou	Wonderful, no thank you	
ゆうめい	Yuumei	Famous	
きれい	Kirei	Pretty, beautiful	
ていねい	teinei	Polite	
きらい	kirai	Dislike	
しずか	shizuka	Quiet	
ひま	hima	free / not busy	
にぎやか	nigiyaka	Lively	
べんり	benri	convenient	

JLPT N5 VOCAB

Practice Quiz 65

な adjectives for N5 (1 -10)

Hiragana	Romaji	Meaning	✓
すき	Suki		
けっこう	Kekkou		
ゆうめい	Yuumei		
きれい	Kirei		
ていねい	teinei		
きらい	kirai		
しずか	shizuka		
ひま	hima		
にぎやか	nigiyaka		
べんり	benri		

な adjectives for N5 (2 -20)

Hiragana	Romaji	Meaning	✓
げんき	genki	Lively, well, energetic	
いろいろ	iroiro	Various	
だいじょうぶ	daijoubu	Ok, well, healthy	
じょうぶ	Joubu	Healthy, robus	
たいへん	Taihen	Terrible, difficult	
らく	Raku	Comfortable, easy	
いや	Iya	Unpleasant	
たいせつ	Taisetsu	Important	
じょうず	jyouzu	Good, skilled	
へた	heta	Bad, unskilled at	

Practice Quiz 66

な adjectives for N5 (2 -20)

Hiragana	Romaji	Meaning	✓
げんき	genki		
いろいろ	iroiro		
だいじょうぶ	daijoubu		
じょうぶ	Joubu		
たいへん	Taihen		
らく	Raku		
いや	Iya		
たいせつ	Taisetsu		
じょうず	jyouzu		
へた	heta		

JLPT N5 VOCAB

な adjectives for N5 (21 -30)

Hiragana	Romaji	Meaning	✓
いっしょうけんめい	isshoukenmei	To ones fullest possibility	
きけん	kiken	Dangerous	
ざんねん	zannen	Regrettable, disappointing	
しんぱい	shinpai	Care, worry	
じゆう	jiyuu	Free, unrestrained	
じゅうぶん	jyuubun	Sufficient	
だいすき	daisuki	Passionate, love	
てきとう	tekitou	Proper, suitable	
とくべつ	Tokubetsu	Special	
ねっしん	nesshin	Eager, enthusiastic	

JLPT N5 VOCAB

Practice Quiz 67

な adjectives for N5 (21 -30)

Hiragana	Romaji	Meaning	✓
いっしょうけんめい	isshoukenmei		
きけん	kiken		
ざんねん	zannen		
しんぱい	shinpai		
じゆう	jiyuu		
じゅうぶん	jyuubun		
だいすき	daisuki		
てきとう	tekitou		
とくべつ	Tokubetsu		
ねっしん	nesshin		

JLPT N5 VOCAB

な adjectives for N5 (31 -36)

Hiragana	Romaji	Meaning	✓
ひつよう	Hitsuyou	Necessary	
まじめ	majime	Serous,earnest	
まっすぐ	massugu	Straight	
むり	muri	Unreasonable, not possible	
りっぱ	Rippa	Excellent, splendid	
びょうき	byouki	to feel sick, unwell	

Practice Quiz 68

な adjectives for N5 (31 -36)

Hiragana	Romaji	Meaning	✓
ひつよう	Hitsuyou		
まじめ	majime		
まっすぐ	massugu		
むり	muri		
りっぱ	Rippa		
びょうき	byouki		

JLPT N5 VOCAB

SECTION 3
N5 VOCABULARY
Verbs

N5 Verbs (1 -10)

Furigana	Romaji	English	✓
はじめ	hajime	start, the beginning	
きえる	kieru	to go out, to vanish	
きく	kiku	to hear, to listen, to ask	
ある	aru	to possess	
あびる	abiru	to take a shower	
あらう	arau	to wash	
そうじ	souji	to clean	
はれる	hareru	to clear up	
みがく	migaku	to polish, to brush	
かける	kakeru	to wear	

Practice Qui 69

N5 Verbs (1 -10)

Furigana	Romaji	English	✓
はじめ	hajime		
きえる	kieru		
きく	kiku		
ある	aru		-
あびる	abiru		
		to wash	-
		to clean	
		to clear up	
		to polish, to brush	
		to wear	

N5 Verbs (11 -20)

Furigana	Romaji	English	✓
かぶる	kaburu	to put on a hat	
きる	kiru	to wear, to put on	
ぬぐ	nugu	to take off clothes	
はく	haku	to put on shoes	
のむ	nomu	to drink	
しぬ	shinu	to die, to pas away	
たべる	taberu	to eat	
かえる	kaeru	to return home	
すむ	sumu	to live, to reside somewhere	
ある	aru	to be, to exist	

Practice Quiz 70

N5 Verbs (11 -20)

Furigana	Romaji	English	✓
かぶる	kaburu		
きる	kiru		
ぬぐ	nugu		
はく	haku		
のむ	nomu		
		to die, to pass away	
		to eat	
		to return home	
		to live, to reside somewhere	
		to be, to exist	

JLPT N5 VOCAB

N5 Verbs (21 -30)

Furigana	Romaji	English	✓
はなす	hanasu	to talk, to speak,	
あそぶ	asobu	to play	
あるく	aruku	to walk	
うたう	utau	to sing	
およぐ	oyogu	to swim	
とる	toru	to take a photo	
なく	naku	to sing, mew, moo	
ひく	hiku	to play (an instrument)	
みせる	miseru	to look, to watch	
みる	miru	to see, to watch	

Practice Quiz 71
N5 Verbs (21 -30)

Furigana	Romaji	English	✓
はなす	hanasu		
あそぶ	asobu		
あるく	aruku		
うたう	utau		
およぐ	oyogu		
		to take a photo	
		to sing, mew, moo	
		to play (an instrument)	
		to look, to watch	
		to see, to watch	

JLPT N5 VOCAB

N5 Verbs (31 -40)

Furigana	Romaji	English	✓
やすむ	yasumu	to rest	
くる	kuru	to come	
さく	saku	to blossom	
かける	kakeru	to make a phone call	
はたらく	hataraku	to work	
つとめる	tsutomeru	to work for someone	
うまれる	umareru	to be born	
なる	naru	to become	
べんきょう	benkyou	to study	
おぼえる	oboeru	to memorize,	

JLPT N5 VOCAB

Practice Quiz 72
N5 Verbs (31 -40)

Furigana	Romaji	English	✓
やすむ	yasumu		
くる	kuru		
さく	saku		
かける	kakeru		
はたらく	hataraku		
		to work for someone	
		to be born	
		to become	
		to study	
		to memorize,	

JLPT N5 VOCAB

N5 Verbs (41 -50)

Furigana	Romaji	English	✓
かく	kaku	to write	
こたえる	kotaeru	to answer	
しる	shiru	to know	
すわる	suwaru	to sit	
ならう	narau	to learn	
ならぶ	narabu	to form a line	
ならべる	naraberu	to line up	
よむ	yomu	to read	
はる	haru	spring	
うる	uru	to sell	

JLPT N5 VOCAB

Practice Quiz 73

N5 Verbs (41 -50)

Furigana	Romaji	English	✓
かく	kaku		
こたえる	kotaeru		
しる	shiru		
すわる	suwaru		
ならう	narau		
		to form a line	
		to line up	
		to read	
		spring	
		to sell	

N5 Verbs (51 -60)

Furigana	Romaji	English	✓
かう	kau	to buy	
かえす	kaesu	to return an object	
はしる	hashiru	to run	
やる	yaru	to do	
おわる	owaru	to end	
かかる	kakaru	to take time	
ねる	neru	to go to bed	
いく	iku	to go	
おりる	oriru	to get off	
しめる	shimeru	to fasten a seatbelt	

Practice Quiz 74
N5 Verbs (51 -60)

Furigana	Romaji	English	✓
かう	kau		
かえす	kaesu		
はしる	hashiru		
やる	yaru		
おわる	owaru		
		to take time,	
		to go to bed	
		to go	
		to get off	
		to fasten a seatbelt	

JLPT N5 VOCAB

N5 Verbs (61 -70)

Furigana	Romaji	English	✓
のぼる	noboru	to climb up	-
のる	noru	to take, to ride	
さす	sasu	to open an umbrella	
ふく	fuku	to blow (wind)	
ふる	furu	to fall (rain, snow)	
かす	kasu	to lend	-
かりる	kariru	to borrow	
あう	au	to meet	
あく	aku	open	
あける	akeru	to open	

JLPT N5 VOCAB

Practice Quiz 75
N5 Verbs (61 -70)

Furigana	Romaji	English	✓
のぼる	noboru		‑
のる	noru		
さす	sasu		
ふく	fuku		
ふる	furu		
		to lend	‑
		to borrow	
		to meet	
		open	
		to open	

JLPT N5 VOCAB

N5 Verbs (71 -80)

Furigana	Romaji	English	✓
あげる	ageru	to give	
いう	iu	to say, to tell	
いる	iru	need, must	
いる	iru	to exist	
いれる	ireru	to insert, to put in	
おきる	okiru	to get up, to stand up	
おく	oku	to put, to place	
おくる	okuru	to send	
おす	osu	to push	
きる	kiru	to cut	

JLPT N5 VOCAB

Practice Quiz 76
N5 Verbs (71 -80)

Furigana	Romaji	English	✓
あげる	ageru		
いう	iu		
いる	iru		
いる	iru		
いれる	ireru		
		to get up, to stand up	
		to put, to place	
		to send	
		to push	
		to cut	

N5 Verbs (81 -90)

Furigana	Romaji	English	✓
けす	kesu	to turn off, switch off	
こまる	komaru	to be in trouble	
しまる	shimaru	to close	
しめる	shimeru	to close	
すう	suu	to breathe, to smoke	
する	suru	to do	
だす	dasu	to take out, hand in	
たつ	tatsu	to stand	
たのむ	tanomu	to ask, to request	
ちがう	chigau	Different	

Practice Quiz 77
N5 Verbs (81 -90)

Furigana	Romaji	English	✓
けす	kesu		
こまる	komaru		
しまる	shimaru		
しめる	shimeru		
すう	suu		
		to do	
		to take out, hand in	
		to stand	
		to ask, to request	
		Different	

N5 Verbs (91 -100)

Furigana	Romaji	English	✓
つかう	tsukau	to use	
つかれる	tsukareru	to get tired	
つく	tsuku	to arrive	
つくる	tsukuru	to make, to produce	
つける	tsukeru	to turn on	
でかける	dekakeru	to go out	
できる	dekiru	can	
でます	demasu	to leave	
とぶ	tobu	to fly	
とまる	tomaru	to stop	

Practice Quiz 78
N5 Verbs (91 -100)

Furigana	Romaji	English	✓
つかう	tsukau		
つかれる	tsukareru		
つく	tsuku		
つくる	tsukuru		
つける	tsukeru		
		to go out	
		can	
		to leave	
		to fly	
		to stop	

JLPT N5 VOCAB

N5 Verbs (101 - 112)

Furigana	Romaji	English	✓
はいる	~~hairu~~	to enter	
はじまる	hajimaru	to begin, to start	
はる	haru	to put on, to stick	
ひく	hiku	to pull	
まがる	magaru	to turn	
まつ	matsu	to wait	
もつ	motsu	to have, to own	
よぶ	yobu	to call	
わかる	wakaru	to know, to understand	
わすれる	wasureru	to forget	
わたす	watasu	to hand over	
わたる	wataru	to cross	

JLPT N5 VOCAB

Practice Quiz 79

N5 Verbs (101 - 112)

Furigana	Romaji	English	✓
はいる	~~hairu~~		
はじまる	hajimaru		
はる	haru		
ひく	hiku		
まがる	magaru		
まつ	matsu		
		to have, to own	
		to call	
		to know, to understand	
		to forget	
		to hand over	
		to cross	

JLPT N5 VOCAB

SECTION 3
N5 VOCABULARY
KANJI

JLPT N5 VOCAB

N5 Kanji (1 – 10)

Kanji	Onyomi	Kunyomi	English	✓
安	AN	yasu(i)	peace, cheap, safety	
一	ICHI, ITSU	hito(tsu), hito-	one	
飲	IN	no(mu)	to drink	
右	U, YUU	migi	right	
雨	U	ame	rain	
駅	EKI	–	station	
円	EN	maru(i)	circle, Yen, round	
火	KA	hi	fire	
花	KA	hana	flower, blossom	
下	KA, GE	shimo, sa(geru),	below, down	

JLPT N5 VOCAB

Practice Quiz 80

N5 Kanji (1 – 10)

Kanji	Onyomi	Kunyomi	English	✓
安				
一				
飲				
右				
雨				
駅				
円				
火				
花				
下				

JLPT N5 VOCAB

N5 Kanji (11 – 20)

Kanji	Onyomi	Kunyomi	English	✓
何	KA	Nani	what, how many, which	
会	KAI, E	a(u)	to meet, to come together, society	
外	GAI, GE	soto, hoka, hazu(reru),	outside, other, disconnect	
学	GAKU	mana(bu)	school, learning	
間	KAN, KEN	aida	time, time span	
気	KI, KE	–	soul, spirit	
九	KYUU, KU	kokono(tsu), kokono-	nine	
休	KYUU	yasu(mu)	to rest	
魚	GYO	sakana, uo	fish	
金	KIN, KON	kane	gold, metal, money	

JLPT N5 VOCAB

Practice Quiz 81
N5 Kanji (11 – 20)

Kanji	Onyomi	Kunyomi	English	✓
何				
会				
外				
学				
間				
気				
九				
休				
魚				
金				

N5 Kanji (21 – 30)

Kanji	Onyomi	Kunyomi	English	✓
空	KUU	sora, a(keru),	sky, empty	
月	GETSU, GATSU	tsuki	month, moon	
見	KEN	mi(ru), mi(eru),	to see, to be visible,	
言	GEN, GON	i(u)	word, to talk	
古	KO	furu(i)	old, used	
五	GO	itsu(tsu), itsu-	five	
後	GO, KOU	ato, oku(reru),	after, later, back,	
午	GO	–	noon	
語	GO	kata(ru), kata(rau)	word, to talk	
校	KOU	–	school	

JLPT N5 VOCAB

Practice Quiz 82

N5 Kanji (21 – 30)

Kanji	Onyomi	Kunyomi	English	✓
空				
月				
見				
言				
古				
五				
後				
午				
語				
校				

JLPT N5 VOCAB

N5 Kanji (31 – 40)

Kanji	Onyomi	Kunyomi	English	✓
口	KOU, KU	kuchi	mouth	
行	KOU	i(ku), yu(ku), okona(u)	to walk. to go, to do, to carry out	
高	KOU	taka(i), taka(maru),	high, expensive,	
国	KOKU	kuni	country	
今	KON, KIN	ima	now	
左	SA	hidari	left	
三	SAN	mit(tsu), mi-	three	
山	SAN	yama	mountain	
四	SHI	yo(ttsu), yu(tsu), yo-	four	
子	SHI, SU	ko	child	

Practice Quiz 83

N5 Kanji (31 – 40)

Kanji	Onyomi	Kunyomi	English	✓
口				
行				
高				
国				
今				
左				
三				
山				
四				
子				

N5 Kanji (41 – 50)

Kanji	Onyomi	Kunyomi	English	✓
耳	JI	mimi	ear	
時	JI	toki	time, hour	
七	SHICHI	nana(tsu), nana-, nano-	seven	
車	SHA	kuruma	car, wheel	
社	SHA	yashiro	shinto shrine, society	
手	SHU	te	hand	
週	SHUU	–	week	
十	JUU, JI	too, to-	ten, cross	
出	SHUTSU	da(su), de(ru)	to leave, to get out.	
書	SHO	ka(ku)	to write	

Practice Quiz 84

N5 Kanji (41 – 50)

Kanji	Onyomi	Kunyomi	English	✓
耳				
時				
七				
車				
社				
手				
週				
十				
出				
書				

N5 Kanji (51 – 60)

Kanji	Onyomi	Kunyomi	English	✓
女	JO, NYO	onna, me	woman, female	
小	SHOU	chii(sai), ko-, o-	small	
少	SHOU	suko(shi), suku(nai)	a little	
上	SHOU, JOU	ue, kami, a(geru),	above, upper	
食	SHOKU	ta(beru), ku(ru),	to eat	
新	SHIN	atara(shii), ara(ta), nii-	new	
人	JIN, NIN	hito	person	
水	SUI	mizu	water	
生	SEI, SHOU	i(kiru), u(mu),	to live, to grow,	
西	SEI, SAI	nishi	west	

Practice Quiz 85
N5 Kanji (51 – 60)

Kanji	Onyomi	Kunyomi	English	✓
女				
小				
少				
上				
食				
新				
人				
水				
生				
西				

N5 Kanji (61 – 70)

Kanji	Onyomi	Kunyomi	English	✓
川	SEN	kawa	river	
千	SEN	chi	thousand	
先	SEN	saki	before, in future	
前	ZEN	mae	before	
足	SOKU	ashi, ta(su)	foot, to add	
多	TA	oo(i)	many	
大	DAI, TAI	ou(kii), oo(i)	big, a lot	
男	DAN, NAN	otoko	man, male	
中	CHUU	naka	inner, center, between	
長	CHOU	naga(i)	long, leader	

JLPT N5 VOCAB

Practice Quiz 86

N5 Kanji (61 – 70)

Kanji	Onyomi	Kunyomi	English	✓
川				
千				
先				
前				
足				
多				
大				
男				
中				
長				

JLPT N5 VOCAB

N5 Kanji (71 – 80)

Kanji	Onyomi	Kunyomi	English	✓
天	TEN	ame, ama	sky	
店	TEN	mise	shop	
電	DEN	–	electricity	
土	DO, TO	tsuchi	earth, ground	
東	TOU	higashi	east	
道	DOU	michi	street, path	
読	DOKU	yo(mu)	to read	
南	NAN	minami	south	
二	NI	futa(tsu), futa-	two	
日	NICHI, JITSU	hi, -ka	day, sun	

JLPT N5 VOCAB

Practice Quiz 87

N5 Kanji (71 – 80)

Kanji	Onyomi	Kunyomi	English	✓
天				
店				
電				
土				
東				
道				
読				
南				
二				
日				

JLPT N5 VOCAB

Kanji N5 (81 – 90)

Kanji	Onyomi	Kunyomi	English	✓
入	NYUU	hai(ru), i(ru), i(reru)	to enter, to insert	
年	NEN	toshi	year	
買	BAI	ka(u)	to buy	
白	HAKU, BYAKU	shiro(i), shiro	white	
八	HACHI	yat(tsu), ya(tsu), ya-, you-	eight	
半	HAN	naka(ba)	half, middle, semi-	
百	HYAKU	–	hundred	
父	FU	chichi	father	
分	BUN, BU, FUN	wa(keru), wa(karu)	part, minute, to understand	
聞	BUN, MON	ki(ku), ki(koeru)	to hear, to listen, to ask	

Practice Quiz 88

Kanji N5 (81 – 90)

Kanji	Onyomi	Kunyomi	English	✓
入				
年				
買				
白				
八				
半				
百				
父				
分				
聞				

N5 Kanji (91 – 102)

Kanji	Onyomi	Kunyomi	English	✓
母	BO	haha	mother	
北	HOKU	kita	north	
木	BOKU, MOKU	ki, ko	tree, wood	
本	HON	moto	book, source, main-	
毎	MAI	–	each, every	
万	MAN, BAN	–	ten thousand, all, many	
名	MEI, MYOU	na	name, reputation	
目	MOKU	me	eye	
友	YUU	tomo	friend	
来	RAI	ku(ru), kita(ru), kita(su)	to come	
立	RITSU	ta(tsu), ta(teru)	to stand, to establish	
話	WA	hanashi, hana(su)	story,	

JLPT N5 VOCAB

Practice Quiz 89

N5 Kanji (91 – 102)

Kanji	Onyomi	Kunyomi	English	✓
母				
北				
木				
本				
毎				
万				
名				
目				
友				
来				
立				
話				

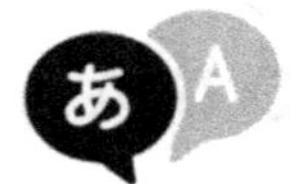

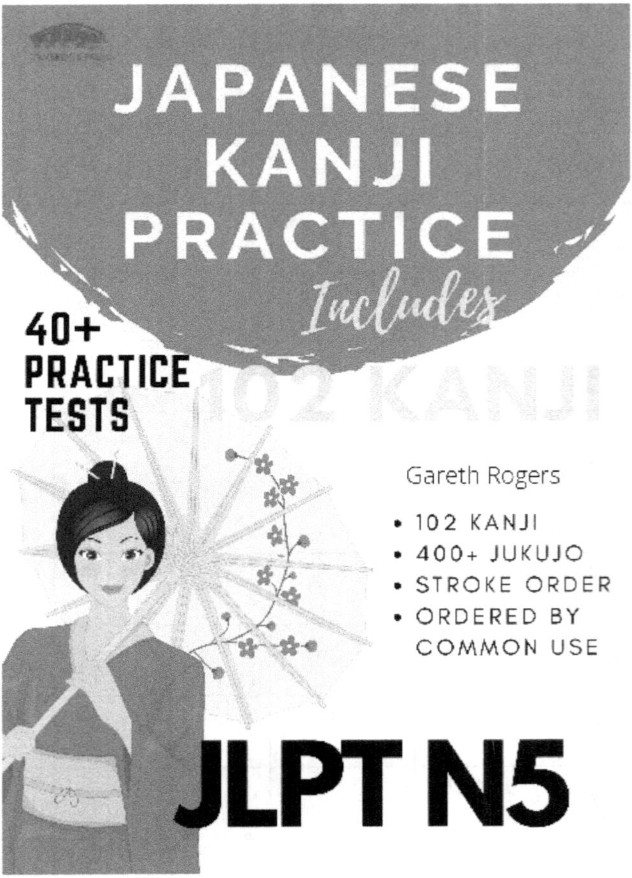
JAPANESE
KANJI
PRACTICE
Includes
102 KANJI
40+
PRACTICE
TESTS
Gareth Rogers
• 102 KANJI
• 400+ JUKUJO
• STROKE ORDER
• ORDERED BY
COMMON USE
JLPT N5

www.ingramcontent.com/pod-product-compliance
Lightning Source LLC
Chambersburg PA
CBHW051104050726
47592CB00002B/666